TROPICAL PINEAPPLE PLANTS

YOU WILL NEED

a slice from the top of a pineapple

a spoon

sand

water

a small bowl

compost

a large plant pot

a clear plastic bag

1

Gently take away the pineapple flesh with the spoon.

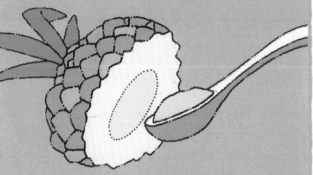

Leave the pineapple top on its side for three days.
The top must dry out.

2

Put the sand in the bowl and make the sand damp.

Stand the pineapple top on the sand.

3

Put the bowl in the plastic bag.

Leave the bag in a warm cupboard for a few weeks.
Make sure you keep the sand damp.

4

When the pineapple top has grown some roots, you can take it out of the cupboard.

Plant it in a pot of damp compost.
Keep the plant warm and damp.

CITRUS PIP PLANTS

YOU WILL NEED

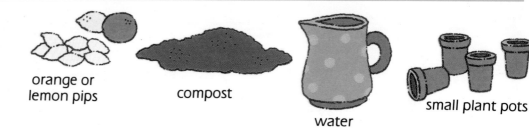

orange or lemon pips

compost

water

small plant pots

1

Fill the plant pots with compost.

2

Use your finger to make holes in the compost.
Drop an orange or lemon pip into each hole and cover up the pips with more compost.

3

Water the compost.

4

Stand the pots in a dark, warm cupboard and keep the compost damp.

5

In a few weeks the little pip trees will start to grow and then you can take them out of the cupboard.

CRESS LETTERS

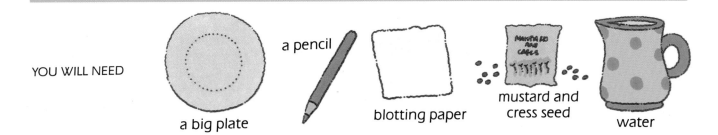

YOU WILL NEED

a big plate

a pencil

blotting paper

mustard and cress seed

water

1

Write a word on the blotting paper.

2

Put the paper on the plate and pour some water on to it.

3

Drop the seeds on to the letters.

4

Keep the blotting paper wet and the seeds will grow into the word.

This plant is safe to eat.

5

AN ONION IN A BOTTLE

YOU WILL NEED

an onion

water

an empty jam jar

1 Fill the jar with water.

2 Stand the round end of the onion in the water.

3 Keep the jar full of water and the onion will grow roots and green shoots.

6

AVOCADO PLANTS

YOU WILL NEED

 an avocado stone

a jar big enough to hold the stone

 water

a bowl

compost

 a plant pot

1

Put the stone into the bowl.

Cover the stone with water and leave it for two days.

2

Fill the jar with water.

Stand the round end of the stone in the top of the jar.

3

Keep the jar full of water. Wait for the stone to split and grow roots and shoots.

4

When the roots and shoots have grown, put the stone in the plant pot full of damp compost.

The compost should cover half of the stone. Keep the compost damp.

A CARROT TOP JUNGLE

YOU WILL NEED

carrot tops

screw top lids

a large plate or tray

soil or sand

water

small toy animals

1 Put the carrot tops in the lids.
Keep the lids full of water.

2 Put the soil on to the plate and press the lids into the soil.

3 Give the carrot tops lots of water.
When the carrot tops have grown lots of leaves, you can put your animals into the jungle.

A PRESSED FLOWER GARDEN

YOU WILL NEED

flowers and leaves

sheets of newspaper

heavy books

a sheet of white paper

glue and a glue brush

crayons

1 Collect some flowers and leaves.

2 Press the flowers and leaves between sheets of newspaper. Put some heavy books on top.

3 Draw a picture of a garden path and a garden pond on a piece of paper. Glue the pressed flowers and leaves on to the garden.

A GARDEN IN A BOTTLE

YOU WILL NEED

 a large empty candy jar

 small stones

 compost a fork

 a cotton reel

 small plants

1

Put the stones in the bottom of the jar.

2

Cover the stones with compost.

3

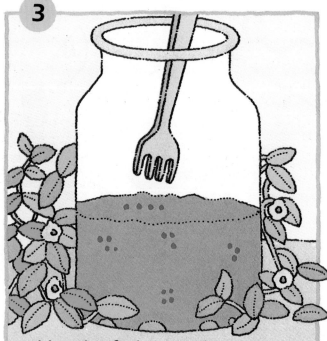

Use the fork to make some holes in the compost.

4

Put the plants in the holes and press the compost round the roots with the cotton reel. Keep the compost damp.

A PLATE GARDEN

YOU WILL NEED

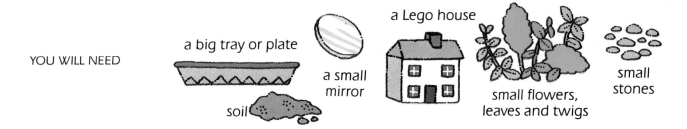

a big tray or plate

a small mirror

soil

a Lego house

small flowers, leaves and twigs

small stones

1 Fill the plate with soil.

2 Put the Lego house on the plate.

Make a small pond by putting the mirror on the soil.

3 Use the flowers, leaves and twigs to make a garden.

11

A SALAD IN A JAR

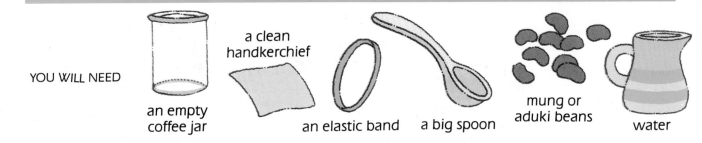

YOU WILL NEED

an empty coffee jar

a clean handkerchief

an elastic band

a big spoon

mung or aduki beans

water

1 Put 2 big spoonfuls of beans in the jar.

2 Pour some water over the beans.

3 Put the handkerchief over the top of the jar and put the elastic band round the top.

Leave the beans for 12 hours.

4 Empty the water out through the handkerchief.

5 Put the jar in a dark place. Every day water the beans and then empty the water out through the handkerchief. The beans take a week to grow.

This plant is safe to eat.

12

DWARF TOMATOES

YOU WILL NEED

a packet of dwarf
bush tomato seeds

plant pots

compost

water

liquid plant
food

1

In the Spring,
fill a large
plant pot with
compost.
Make some
holes in the
compost with
your finger and
drop a seed
into each hole.

2

Keep the
seeds
watered and
when the
seedlings are
5cm high put
each one into
its own pot.

3

Let the plants grow on a sunny
window-sill and give them
plenty of liquid food and water.

4

Soon you will have lots of small
tomatoes for a salad.

**The tomatoes are safe to
eat.**

DATES

YOU WILL NEED  3 date stones 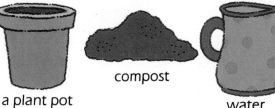 a plant pot compost water a clear plastic bag

1 Put the date stones into the plant pot full of compost.

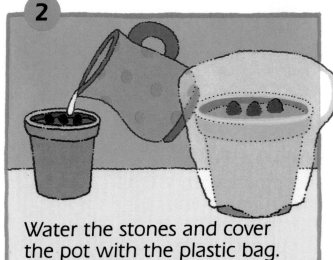

2 Water the stones and cover the pot with the plastic bag.

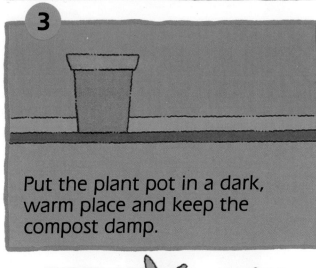

3 Put the plant pot in a dark, warm place and keep the compost damp.

4 When the little date plants have grown, you can take away the plastic bag and put them into a light place. Keep the little plants warm.

A DESERT IN A BOWL

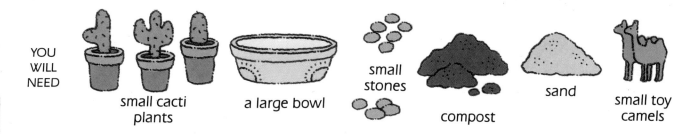

YOU WILL NEED

small cacti plants

a large bowl

small stones

compost

sand

small toy camels

1 Put the stones in the bottom of the bowl.

2 Cover the stones with compost and sand
Put some sand on top of the compost and sand.

3 Plant the cacti 10cm apart and put the camels in the desert.

PREPARING YOUR OUTDOOR GARDEN

YOU WILL NEED a bucket a spade a fork

1

In October see how many stones and weeds you can pick up from your patch of garden. Put the stones and weeds into a bucket.

2

Use the spade to dig all over your garden.

3

Use the fork to break up the big lumps of soil.
The Winter weather will help to get the soil ready for planting in the Spring.

PLANTING FLOWER SEEDS

a bucket

a fork

a rake

a watering can

flower seeds such as
Pansies, Cornflowers,
Marigolds or Nasturtiums

1

In the Spring use the fork to
dig all over your garden.
Put any stones or weeds into
the bucket.
Rake the soil until it is very fine.

2

The day before sowing your
seeds, water the soil.

Sprinkle the seeds on to the
soil and cover them gently with
the rake.

3

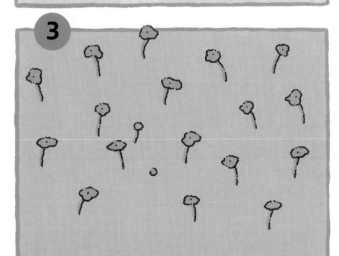

When the seedlings are 2cm
high, pull some of them out.
This will leave the others with
more room to grow.

4

Keep the seedlings watered
and pull out any weeds.
In a few weeks you will have
some flowers.

HANGING BASKETS

YOU WILL NEED

a wire hanging basket

pieces of moss

compost

seedling plants such as Lobelia, Nasturtium, Petunia, Sweet pea.

a watering can

1

Cover the inside of the basket with the pieces of moss.

2

Fill the basket with the compost and then plant the seedlings.

3

Water the basket and hang it on a sunny wall.
Keep the compost damp.

4

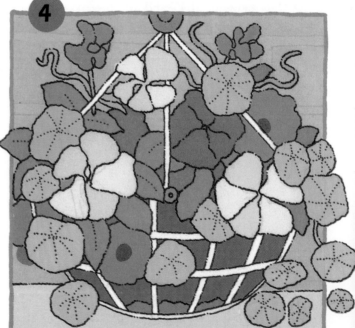

In a few weeks your basket will be filled with flowers.

18

INITIAL A MARROW

YOU WILL NEED

marrow (Summer squash) seedlings

a watering can

a long nail

1

Plant the seedlings in May in a warm, sunny spot.
They should be put about 60cm apart.

2

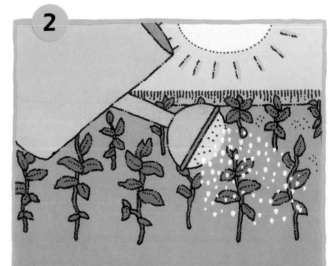

Water the seedlings every day.

3

When the baby marrows are very small, gently cut your name on to the skin of the marrow with the nail.

4

As the marrow grows bigger, so will your name.

This plant is safe to eat.

A SALAD BOWL GARDEN

YOU WILL NEED

a stick

a rake

a packet of radish seeds

a packet of lettuce seeds

a watering can

1

In the Springtime rake the soil and pull up any weeds.

2
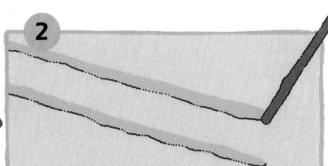
Make two long lines in the soil with the stick. The lines need to be 20cm apart.

3

Put the radish seeds in one line and the lettuce seeds in the second line. Gently rake the soil over the seeds.

4

Water the seeds and when the seedlings are 3cm high pull some of them out. This will give the others room to grow.

5
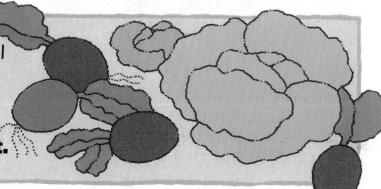
The radish will be ready to pull up after 3 weeks and the lettuce will be ready to eat after 4 weeks.

These plants are safe to eat.

GLAZED GOURDS

YOU WILL NEED

 a packet of mixed Cucurbita seeds

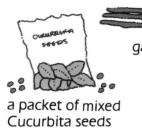 garden canes

string

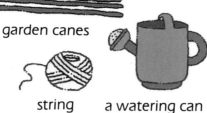 a watering can

a rake

 a soft cloth

clear varnish and a paint brush

 a pretty basket

1

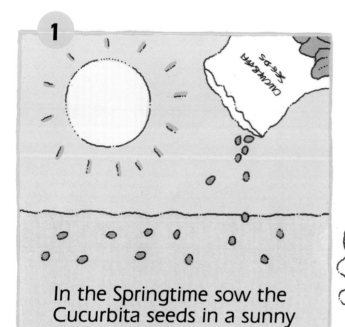

In the Springtime sow the Cucurbita seeds in a sunny patch of garden.

2

Water the seeds every day.

Put the garden canes in the soil and help the plants to climb up the canes by fastening them with string.

3

Pick the gourds on a warm sunny day and put them on a window sill to dry out.

4

Polish the gourds with the cloth and then paint them with a coat of varnish.

When they are dry, put them together in the pretty basket.

A SUNFLOWER RACE

YOU WILL NEED

a packet of
giant sunflower
(Helianthus) seeds

long garden canes

a watering can

string

name tags and
a marker pen

1

Give each of your friends two
or three sunflower seeds.
Plant them in a sunny spot in
the garden about 60cm apart.
Put a name tag by each seed.

2

Water the seeds every day.

3

Sunflowers
grow very
quickly and
they can grow
up to over
3 metres.
You will need
to tie the
sunflowers to
the garden
canes to stop
them falling
over.

4

Decide on a judging day during
the late Summer and give a
prize to the person with the
tallest sunflower.

A RUNNER BEAN WIG-WAM

YOU WILL NEED

3 very long
garden sticks

6 runner bean seeds

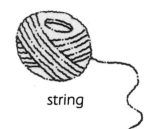

string

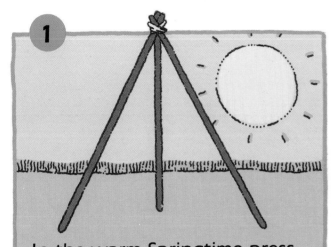

1

In the warm Springtime press
the sticks into the ground to
make a triangle.
Ask a grown up to tie the tops
of the sticks together.

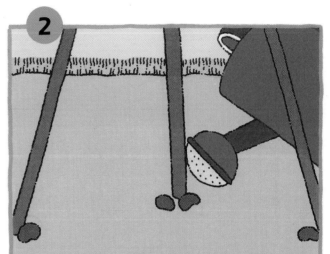

2

Plant one seed on each side of
each stick.
Water the seeds.

3

As the plants grow, help them
to curl up around the sticks.
When the plants have flowers,
spray them with water.

4

When the beans have grown
have beans for dinner every
few days. The more you pick
the more will grow!

The beans are safe to eat

GROWING YOUR NAME

YOU WILL NEED

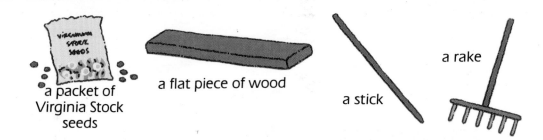

a packet of
Virginia Stock
seeds

a flat piece of wood

a stick

a rake

1

In the Spring rake the soil and pull out any weeds.

2

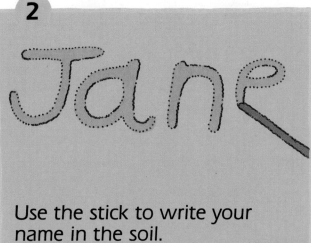

Use the stick to write your name in the soil.

3

Sprinkle the seeds along the letters. Gently press the seeds into the ground with the flat piece of wood. Do not put soil on top of the seeds.

4

Wait a few weeks and watch your name grow.